INTERACTIVE **WORKBOOK**

SHATTERING THE SHAME™

*A Guide to Breaking Free From
the Shame of CSA*

Thank you to Theresa Harvard Johnson for your contribution to *Shattering the Shame*.

BOOKLOGIX
Alpharetta, GA

The resources contained within this book are provided for informational purposes only and should not be used to replace the specialized training and professional judgment of a healthcare or mental healthcare professional. Angela's Voice and the publisher of this work cannot be held responsible for the use of the information provided. Always consult a licensed mental health professional before making any decision regarding treatment of yourself or others.

Copyright © 2014, 2023 by Angela's Voice

Second Edition

All rights reserved. No part of this book may be reproduced or transmitted in any form or by any means, electronic or mechanical, including photocopying, recording, or any information storage and retrieval system, without permission in writing from the author.

ISBN: 978-1-61005-986-2

This ISBN is the property of BookLogix for the express purpose of sales and distribution of this title. The content of this book is the property of the copyright holder only. BookLogix does not hold any ownership of the content of this book and is not liable in any way for the materials contained within. The views and opinions expressed in this book are the property of the Author/Copyright holder, and do not necessarily reflect those of BookLogix.

∞ This paper meets the requirements of ANSI/NISO Z39.48-1992 (Permanence of Paper)

Author, Angela Williams, MFP
Co-Author, Theresa Harvard Johnson
Design and Illustration by Mark Sandlin
Design production by Felicia Kahn

Dedication

Shattering the Shame™ *is dedicated to Isabella, a 4-month-old child who was raped and killed in 2014, and to all the wounded warriors of child sexual abuse.*

CONTENTS

Introduction to Shattering the Shame _____ 1

Defining Shame _____ 2

Shame Steals _____ 4

Societal Stigma _____ 7

Shame on Them _____ 10

Invisible Survivors _____ 13

The Victim _____ 15

Sickness of Shame _____ 17

Shame Based Identity _____ 22

Blame of Shame _____ 26

Shame of Physical Response _____ 30

Masking the Shame _____ 32

The Shame of Feeling Unclean _____ 35

Shame Solutions _____ 36

Overcoming Shame-Based Thinking _____ 38

Challenge Shame-Based Thoughts _____ 42

Collateral Damage _____ 43

A Mother's Shame _____ 45

Faith as a Tool to Overcome Shame _____ 47

Compassion Calls _____ 49

Smile _____ 50

Healing in Community _____ 51

Voice of Action _____ 52

Angela's Voice _____ 54

Join the Angela's Voice Movement _____ 56

INTRODUCTION

If there was one thing nearly all survivors of child sexual abuse (CSA) have experienced at some point in their lives, it is the overpowering and suffocating effects of shame. This workbook, *Shattering the Shame*™, was written specifically to help the survivors of CSA
1) gain a solid understanding of shame,
2) examine how shame may be impacting their lives, and
3) help them overcome the effects of shame while taking critical strategic steps toward embracing a healthier lifestyle.

Having worked with thousands of survivors over the years, Angela's Voice has witnessed the paralyzing impact of shame in the lives of men, women and children worldwide. We understand the chronic struggle many face to overcome its devastating effects. Our greatest desire is to help as many survivors as we can gain freedom from the unhealthy patterns and behaviors imprinted in their hearts and souls as a result of the weight shame dumps upon them.

We applaud you who have the courage to confront shame issues in your own life. We also commend those of you who seek to learn as much as possible in order to better understand where your loved one may be and how you may help in their healing process. As you begin this journey, remember that the emotional trauma and aftermath of CSA is often difficult to tackle all at once. As a result, we must view the healing process like peeling back an onion: one layer at a time. Shame is a layer which can weave its way into the core of a survivor's life, resulting in self-destruction.

As you move through this workbook, you will read true testimonies from men and women who have broken their silence and confronted shame. It is our hope that their testimonies will encourage you in the midst of your journey, empower you to break the silence within your own life, and shatter the shame. We are grateful to those who have invested in your healing by boldly sharing how the shame of CSA has impacted their lives. As you read their stories, it is our hope that you will be comforted and affirmed in knowing that you are not alone on this healing journey and that one day, you will be able to help others in the midst of their journey.

Please take the time to carefully process and answer the questions, and complete the exercises at the end of each section. Our hope is that layer by layer, piece by piece, and word by word you will begin shattering the shame in your life.

DEFINING SHAME

At some point in life, most of us have experienced shame. Perhaps you were embarrassed by something simple, like falling in public, or as common as losing your train of thought during a speech in front of an audience. While these examples may be a form of shame, they do not adequately express the depth of the emotion that it conveys, especially as it relates to CSA.

In an article published on child maltreatment, shame is described as "a negative and disturbing emotional experience involving feelings of self-condemnation and the desire to hide the damaged self from others."[1] It is seen as a state in which "the whole self feels defective, often as a result of a perceived failure to meet social and self-imposed standards."[2] Further, Dr. Joseph Burgo defines shame as a "painful feeling arising from the consciousness of something dishonorable, improper, and ridiculous" done by oneself or by something done to you.[3]

Other terms that accurately describe shame are *severe humiliation* and *crippling embarrassment.* The impact of shame resulting from CSA can be so devastating and traumatizing that "survivors tend to display more self-destructive behaviors and experience more suicidal ideation than those who have not been abused."[4] Excerpts from a report by the American Counseling Association state the following.

---

1 Feiring, C., & Taska, L. S. (2005, October 4). The Persistence of Shame Following Sexual Abuse: A Longitudinal Look at Risk and Recovery. *The Persistence of Shame Following Sexual Abuse: A Longitudinal Look at Risk and Recovery.* Retrieved May 26, 2014, from http://cmx.sagepub.com/content/10/4/337
2 Ibid.
3 Dr. Joseph Burgo, (2013, May 30). The Difference Between Guilt and Shame. Retrieved May 26, 2014, from http://www.psychologytoday.com/blog/shame/201305/the-difference-between-guilt-and-shame
4 M. Hall, & J. Hall (2011). The long-term effects of childhood sexual abuse: Counseling implications. Retrieved from http://counselingoutfitters.com/vistas/vistas11/Article_19.pdf

"Childhood sexual abuse infringes on the basic rights of human beings. The nature and dynamics of sexual abuse and sexually abusive relationships are often traumatic. When sexual abuse occurs in childhood, it can hinder normal social growth and be a cause of many different psychosocial problems (Maltz, 2002). Childhood sexual abuse has been correlated with higher levels of depression, guilt, shame, self-blame, eating disorders, somatic concerns, anxiety, dissociative patterns, repression, denial, sexual problems, and relationship problems. Depression has been found to be the most common long-term symptom among survivors. Survivors may have difficulty in externalizing the abuse, thus thinking negatively about themselves (Hartman et al., 1987)."[5]

From these definitions, we see that shame can take away everything good a person may have thought about themselves or considered good and decent, and replaces it with thoughts and *beliefs* rooted in insecurity and inferiority. Have you ever wondered why shame seems to have such an impact in the lives of others or why so many people are overcome by shame? It's simple really.

At the very core of our humanity is a desire to be useful, accepted, loved and connected to others. Our humanity longs for and thrives from positive interaction and intimacy. When shame is introduced, it dismantles that usefulness, acceptance, love and the ability to connect with others. It erodes the identity and creates a new belief system with self-hatred, rejection and even self-rejection at the core. It sucks the very life out of its victim's view of their worth and value. It causes a person to fixate and enter into what is commonly called *shame-based* thinking. This type of thinking causes victims to feel they are holding a sign that says, "I am defective and everyone can see it."

At Angela's Voice we have heard many survivors describe themselves as broken, flawed, unclean, unlovable, unimportant, insignificant and weak, and a host of other lies brought on by shame. Shame is an emotion that grows gradually and intensifies over time. Ultimately, its victims become consumed by it and embrace a false perception of who they are and their value. Shame shatters.

---

[5] Ibid.

SHAME STEALS

SHATTERING THE SHAME

As a little girl I remember my first day of kindergarten vividly. When I walked into the brightly colored classroom, with smiling teachers and the sound of nursery tunes playing in the background, my face flushed and my stomach surged up into my throat. I did not understand the meaning of shame, but I do remember gazing around the room and feeling different, embarrassed, and wanting to be invisible. The laughter was piercing and foreign as I remember thinking I have never laughed like that. The childhood glee was elusive and almost insulting. At five years old I felt that everyone who looked in my eyes saw the perversion I had been exposed to and forced to engage in. I felt dirty and damaged. Today, I continue to peel the layers of shame away.

Angela's story represents the experiences of millions of men, women and children who are overcoming the effects of CSA. Shame is one of the primary reasons why 1 in 10 children never report their abuse.[6] Children are manipulated, groomed and violated in such a cunning way that they do not have the words to describe their confusion, violation and humiliation. And let's face the reality: rarely is a child asked if anyone has touched their private parts or if they have been asked to touch the private parts of others.

Imagine Angela as a five year old whose days should have been filled with swinging, playing dress up, catching fireflies on a summer evening, enjoying a bicycle ride, coloring pages and playing hide and go seek. This was the window from which she, and millions of children like her, should have viewed life. Tragically, her innocence was shattered at age three; and by age five there was no frame of reference by which to measure what had happened to her and what she was feeling internally. There must have been signs, symptoms and odd behaviors, but no one asked questions or intervened. Had they asked, would she have told? Probably not, because the fear of retribution was fierce. For fourteen years everyone in her life looked the other way. **Shame stole Angela's childhood.**

---

[6] Statistics-Child Sexual Abuse. Parents for Meagan's Law and The Crime Victims Center. Accessed May 26, 2014. http://www.parentsformeganslaw.org/public/statistics_childSexualAbuse.html

A therapist from Arizona wrote the following.

"Shame is a fear-based internal state of being, accompanied by beliefs of being unworthy and basically unlovable. Shame is a primary emotion that conjures up brief, intense painful feelings and a fundamental sense of inadequacy. Shame experiences bring forth beliefs of 'I am a failure' and 'I am bad' which are a threat to the integrity of the self. This perceived deficit of being bad is so humiliating and disgraceful that there is a need to protect and hide the flawed self from others. Fears of being vulnerable, found out, exposed and further humiliated are paramount. Feelings of shame shut people down so that they can distance themselves from the internal painful state of hopelessness."[7]

Angela not only felt she had done something wrong, but she felt flawed as a human being. She felt different, standing in the middle of that blissful kindergarten class, a member of the class in location externally, yet on the outside looking in, internally. In this country, the median age of CSA is nine. On February 24, 2014, a 4-month-old girl was raped and killed in Albuquerque, New Mexico by a 19-year-old man.[8] Children are vulnerable at all ages.

---

7 Lynne Namka, Ed. D. Shame: The Disowned Part of the Self. (1997) Talk, Trust and Feel Therapeutics. Accessed May 26, 2014. http://www.angriesout.com/teach8.htm

8 Mike Springer. Badly Abused 4 Month Old Dies from Injuries. KOAT Albuquerque. Accessed May 26, 2014. http://www.koat.com/news/new-mexico/albuquerque/badly-abused-baby-dies-from-injuries/24642270

Nearly 30 percent of child sexual assault victims identified by child protective service agencies are between four and seven years of age.[9] And, like for Angela, there is no frame of reference for any child, regardless of age, to place such a horrendous act against them into perspective. Children are powerless with no means of protection.

Consider these questions:

1. How has the shame of CSA impacted your life?

2. How can a child adequately express what they have endured?

3. How is a child expected to process what has happened to him or her?

4. How can they be expected to heal in a silenced society?

5. How old were you when your innocence was violated?

6. When do you think you first identified with feelings of shame in your life?

---

9   Statistics-Child Sexual Abuse. Parents for Meagan's Law and The Crime Victims Center. Accessed May 26, 2014. http://www.parentsformeganslaw.org/public/statistics_childSexualAbuse.html

SOCIETAL STIGMA

SHATTERING THE SHAME: 12-YEAR-OLD BREANN'S STORY

A year after I was molested by my grandfather, my school had an essay contest. The subject was, "My Greatest Fear." I had decided that I was ready to tell my story. With my teacher's help, I wrote about what happened to me during my visit to my grandparents in Michigan. That was huge for me, because I was so scared, but something within me needed to get it out. My bravery was met with opposition. Soon after submitting my essay, my mom received a call from the school counselor. My essay would not be submitted for the contest. It was considered graphic and explicit. When my mom told me the news, I became so angry. I didn't want to tell anyone else again and closed up. What was the point? But my mom wouldn't let me give up. She found Angela's Voice and contacted them. They allowed me to submit it to their website. When Angela's Voice was willing to post my essay, I felt joyful and free. I was able to finally have a voice and not be silenced, which made me feel like I had something to be ashamed of.

In the article, *Eliminating the Stigma of Child Sexual Abuse*, the author writes: "As a society, we shy away when survivors speak about their abusive experiences. Victims are silenced individually in exam and consulting rooms when medical and mental health professionals fail to ask, "Have you ever been a victim of sexual abuse?" and institutionally through religious, youth-serving organizations or schools that tolerate, even cover-up abuse (e.g. Penn State, Catholic Church, Boy Scouts, USA Gymnastics, amoung many others). We need to do better as a society when it comes to facing and ending childhood sexual abuse."[10] Experts agree that CSA remains a taboo subject that very few people want to discuss, acknowledge or assist in finding a solution.

---

10   Silvia M. Dutchevici, MA, LCSW. Eliminating the Stigma of Childhood Sexual Abuse. GoodTherapy.org. (July 17, 2012). Accessed May 26, 2014. http://www.goodtherapy.org/blog/stigma-childhood-sexual-abuse-0717124

This lack of acknowledgment or interest causes survivors, like 12-year-old Breann, to experience *extreme shame* and discouragement. As survivors, many of you can identify with the kind of courage it took Breann to write her story and then decide to share it with her school. For Breann, this was a positive step in her healing journey and an opportunity to empower other children to come forth. The response from her school is a classic example of the kind of response society offers its most vulnerable victims. Had she submitted an essay on dealing with cancer, overcoming an eating disorder or bullying, it would have been a welcomed and celebrated topic. The question before us right now is this, *Why is sharing about her victimization by a family member not a welcomed topic?*

Dr. Ronald C. Summit wrote, "Child victims of sexual abuse face secondary trauma in the crisis of discovery. Their attempts to reconcile their private experiences with the realities of the outer world are assaulted by the disbelief, blame and rejection they experience from adults. The normal coping behavior of the child contradicts the entrenched beliefs and expectations typically held by adults, stigmatizing the child with charges of lying, manipulating or imagining from parents, courts and clinicians. Such abandonment by the very adults most crucial to the child's protection and recovery drives the child deeper into self-blame, self-hate, alienation and re-victimization."[11]

Breann exhibited great courage in her desire to share her greatest fear in a school essay and was met with rejection. She talked about how she never wanted to share again after her experience with the school. Without the support and encouragement of her mother, the "shame-thinking" could have been further engraved in Breann's thinking, affirming the lies associated with it. Social stigma nearly silenced Breann's voice.

Because of the silent stand society has taken concerning CSA, there are few safe places to disclose, and limited understanding concerning how to properly relate, respond or even assist someone in their healing process. We find few if any prevention initiatives geared specifically toward CSA in schools, doctors' offices, churches and youth-serving organizations. In addition, society fails to equip children with understanding what is appropriate or inappropriate behavior between children and adults, the words needed to disclose CSA; and action steps to take when confronting abuse.

---

[11] Roland C. Summit, The child sexual abuse accommodation syndrome, Child Abuse & Neglect, Volume 7, Issue 2, 1983, Pages 177-193, ISSN 0145-2134, http://dx.doi.org/10.1016/0145-2134(83)90070-4. (http://www.sciencedirect.com/science/article/pii/0145213483900704)

If CSA has taken your voice, your power and ultimately your joy, it is not your fault. Any form of sexual assault is an act of violence primarily motivated out of anger. The perpetrators feel the need to control, dominate and humiliate their victims. The blame for assault rests solely on the offender, the person committing the crime – not their victims.

Have you experienced societal stigma? If so, share your experience. _____
_____
_____
_____

When you think of societal stigmas concerning CSA, what are some of the first things that come to your mind? _____
_____
_____
_____

What do you believe can be done to change societal stigmas concerning CSA? _____
_____
_____
_____

SHAME ON THEM

SHATTERING THE SHAME: JESSICA'S STORY

I remember the first time I was forced to participate in a sex act. I was sitting on her knees rocking, nauseous, crying profusely and begging my abusers not to make me participate in or watch what they were doing. I was sickened by the scene being enacted before me, and later by pornographic videos and magazine images. I can still remember the nauseated feeling that overwhelmed me through the entire ordeal. Though I reported what was happening to me, I was accused of stirring up trouble and misunderstanding or misinterpreting what had happened. I was simply told, "Children like to explore their bodies and experiment. That's all. You probably liked it anyway." Well, I didn't like it. Those were teenagers, not little children. I was told to never speak of it again because it might get some good people in real trouble and that the destruction of those relationships would be my fault. For the next eleven years the abuse would escalate and I would suffer in silence until child protective services intervened. But by then, the years of abuse had destroyed any hint of the innocent little girl. Only an angry, bitter, shell of a teenager remained, one who lived in a world of deep depression, self-hatred and shame controlled by medication.

Shame belongs to the perpetrator. Shame belongs to those who have the power to protect a child but choose to do nothing. Shame never ever rests on the shoulder of the victims. **Shame on them.**

Another aspect of shame is called "shaming." Shaming is a form of emotional abuse that can be best described as the malicious act of causing others to experience humiliation and degradation. One of the primary purposes of shaming is to instill fear in a child, and ultimately control them. In an article published by Psychology Today, the author wrote:

"There are many different ways we shame others: Sarcasm, name-calling, expressing disgust, and eye-rolling are all ways we communicate that someone else is not worthy of our respect. Shaming behaviors make us feel superior to that other person, as well as communicate to them that we wish they'd be or act differently, without us having to actually talk to them in an adult way and take responsibility for our own feelings. The same way teasing is so often rooted in hostility, shame takes its energy from judgment and self-righteousness. Shame, in whatever form it takes, is a way to control the other person by using their deeply ingrained need for connection to threaten them with disconnection. It's genius. And nefarious."[12]

Those who sexually abuse children use shame and fear to bind the victim to them and isolate them from others who might help them. The victim is left feeling alone, isolated and very different from everyone around them. Victims describe this as a surreal feeling to see other kids leading normal lives all around them, but feel so different and separate from them due to the abuse they have endured. This shame and silence can last for decades."[13] Shaming is clearly a form of bullying, manipulation and especially control.

When shame is operating in a person's life, it impacts their view of the world and can cripple proper interactions within that world. A survivor's inner voice might recant these beliefs: "The world is not safe. I can't trust anyone. There is something terribly wrong with me." At Angela's Voice, these are all comments we have heard repeated many times by survivors.

---

12   Melissa Kirk. Shame on You! Do You Use Shame to Control Others?, Psychology Today, June 26, 2011. Accessed May 26, 2014. http://www.psychologytoday.com/blog/test-case/201106/shame-you-do-you-use-shame-control-others
13   Common Victim Behaviors of Child Sexual Abuse. The PCAR Pinnacle. March 26, 2013. Accessed May 26, 2014. http://www.pcar.org/blog/common-victim-behaviors-survivors-sexual-abuse

Survivors are often disillusioned concerning their role in this horrific trauma. We can easily say that the shame belongs to them because sexual predators:

- recruit children by deception. They deliberately set out to build a trusting relationship with them, their loved ones and close friends for the sole purpose of making it easier to harm them.
- use manipulative tactics like gift giving, compliments, game play and such to gain access to children and convince them to keep secrets.
- typically plan their sexual assaults. CSA generally "does not just happen." Preparation has gone into plans to abuse that child.
- do absolutely nothing accidentally. Literally every move they make or step that is taken to manipulate a child is deliberate.

These tactics and more are best known as "grooming" techniques. Survivors are encouraged to really grasp an understanding of this so they can clearly see in this instance that shame does not belong to them, but to the perpetrator.

In Jessica's story, she was not only sexually abused, but accused of causing trouble by the caregivers who should have protected her. This is yet another picture of what a silent society might look like; and how blame that rests squarely with the abuser can be dumped on the victim. Not only are Jessica's perpetrators to blame, but so is the caregiver who failed to protect her.

Did someone attempt to shift the blame of your abuse onto you? If so, share your story.

_____
_____
_____
_____
_____
_____
_____
_____
_____

How did you respond? _____

_____

_____

_____

_____

_____

_____

_____

INVISIBLE SURVIVORS

It is easy to see how many brave survivors believe they are invisible; walking along in the shadows of life. Statistics show that many survivors are indeed walking alone, as the world around them looks the other way.

The Centers for Disease Control and Prevention[14] reported that:

- 1 in 4 girls will be sexually abused by age 18
- 1 in 6 boys will be sexually abused by age 18
- Median age of abuse is 9 years old
- Only 1 in 10 will ever tell
- 70% of all sexual assaults in the United States happen to a child
- One sex offender abuses an average of 117 victims
- 93% of abuse is from someone the child knows

14 Centers for Disease Control and Prevention

According to stats from the Bureau of Justice, 93 percent of juvenile sexual assault victims know their attacker, 34.2 percent of their attackers were family members, 58.7 percent were acquaintances, and only 7 percent were strangers.[15]

Society, for the most part, remains oblivious to these statistics and would debate their validity. The truth is, there are people all around you who have been sexually abused as a child, even family members, and many of them are hiding their pain. From research we know there are a reported 42 million (not including those **not** reported) survivors in the United States. Those numbers speak volumes to the fact that surely you are not alone.

For many survivors of CSA, invisibility is equivalent to isolation and dissociation. Isolation in this sense, can be viewed as a complete separation from intimate relationships as well as from society. Dissociation is when a person completely disconnects with what has happened to them. It is commonly called "checking out." Survivors can initiate self-isolation or succumb to varying forms of exclusion; especially within families that refuse to accept what has happened. In the book, *Caring for Sexually Abused Children: A Handbook for Families & Churches*, author R. Timothy Kearney writes: "A move toward isolation can come from the side of the abused child and his or her family as well. Children may see themselves as damaged or different. Many believe that they somehow look different or that they are now bad or tainted."[16]

Isolation speaks immensely to silence, however, it can only be broken when the survivor takes that first step to open up, once in a safe place. Health professionals recommend talking with a counselor or therapist or joining a support group specifically for sexual abuse in order to break isolation. From that point, it is recommended they take steps to trust again by reaching out to people they know or believe may be safe. A pamphlet for survivors of sexual assault states: "Having someone to talk to about how you are feeling may help you to deal with the emotions you are experiencing. Additionally, a counselor can help you express your needs to others and learn how to get those needs met."[17]

---

15   Bureau of Justice Statistics, U.S. Department of Justice, 2000.
16   Kearney, R. T. (2001). Caring for sexually abused children: a handbook for families & churches. Downers Grove, Ill.: InterVarsity Press, 65.
17   After Sexual Assault: A Recovery guide for Survivors. Safe Horizons. http://www.safehorizon.org/images/uploads/misc/1272296041_After_Sexual_Assault_Bklt.pdf

It is fully possible for survivors to begin reconnecting with those around them and moving from invisible to visible.

Have you ever felt your pain was invisible to the world? _____

How many survivors of child sexual abuse do you know? _____

Have you experienced another survivor disclosing their sexual abuse after you have shared your story of abuse? _____

How did you feel? _____

THE VICTIM

SHATTERING THE SHAME: NANETTE'S STORY

Before the age of ten I had been sexually abused by more people than I can count on one hand. I have had a relationship with God since I can remember, talking to Him even as a little girl. I never asked God why all of those things were happening to me because as far as my little girl-self believed, I knew why: because I was bad. Until around the age of 17, I prayed every night before I went to bed and the prayer would always go something like this: "God please protect our home from fires, robbers, tornados and anything else bad." Then my prayer voice would grow a little fainter as I whispered, "And God please, please forgive me for what I have done." "What I have done" encompassed my badness. It encompassed every sexual thing I had done in my childhood. Not once, at any point did I see myself as a victim. I always, to the very core of me, believed I was bad and the things I had done were my fault. I have friends who say they forgot the abuse for many years. I never forgot. It was a shameful secret I carried with me in everything I did.

Shame makes it difficult for survivors of CSA to see themselves as victims. Often, victims view themselves as willing participants in their abuse, and the shaming that comes from the perpetrator and our silent society reinforces this false belief. Nanette's story is a classic example of this.

Nanette, like millions of other survivors, took on the guilt and shame of her abuse and the "bad girl" identity it pressed upon her. The truth remains that Nanette was a victim of a heinous, reviling crime. It is important that survivors understand that a victim is defined as "a person injured or killed as a result of a crime, accident, or other event or action, or a person who has come to feel helpless and passive in the face of misfortune or ill-treatment."[18] In the scope of this definition, CSA survivors are clearly persons injured as a result of a crime.

A perpetrator, however, is someone who brings about or carries out a crime or a deception.[19] It is a person who produces, performs or executes a crime.[20] Victims of CSA generally do not fall into this category. We will talk about the underlying effects of this as we move deeper into this workbook. In the midst of their healing, survivors of CSA grow to understand that someone else was responsible for their pain.

Are you able to see yourself as a victim in light of this understanding? Why or why not?

_____
_____
_____
_____
_____
_____

---

18   Victim. http://www.merriam-webster.com/dictionary/victim
19   Perpetrator. http://www.merriam-webster.com/dictionary/perpetrator
20   Ibid.

What do you believe about your abuse? _____

_____

_____

_____

Who do you feel is responsible for your abuse? _____

_____

SICKNESS OF SHAME

SHATTERING THE SHAME: JESSE'S STORY

I spent eight weeks as an inpatient at a local psychiatric facility after my first suicide attempt at age 17. I was diagnosed with post-traumatic stress disorder, clinical depression and was undergoing further tests for mental illness. I was hearing voices on a regular basis, and experiencing a constant stream of really high highs, and frightening lows. I had developed a violent temper, and on several occasions those behaviors had serious consequences. I had also started hearing voices telling me I was worthless, useless and should just take my own life. I blamed the spiral downturn concerning my life on mental health. It never dawned on me that I was reeling from the effects of child sexual abuse. I was so ashamed by my past that I had created this entirely different life; one in which (I thought) that little girl had long been buried in my deepest thoughts. I reinvented the "Jesse" that everyone around me respected and loved, and lived in that façade for years. I never talked about my past outwardly. People only knew the "me" I presented. But by the time I was 28 years old, I was no longer able to maintain that lie; coping in any capacity was impossible. My meds weren't working. The voices had intensified. I was struggling to get out of bed in the morning, and anger was eating me alive. It was in the midst of another failed suicide attempt that true intervention came, and I began my long journey toward healing.

Lynne Namka wrote: "Shame is the shaper of symptoms, said Donald Nathanson. The unacknowledged thoughts and feelings become repressed and surface later through substitute emotions and dysfunctional behavior. Other emotions are substituted to hide the shame and maintain self-esteem. Anger, depression, exaggerated pride, anxiety and helplessness are substituted to keep from feeling the total blackness of being bad. The buried shame is expressed through defense mechanisms that shield negative unconscious material from surfacing."[21]

Nathanson's summation of the symptoms of shame convey fully what was happening in Jesse's life. Survivors of CSA struggle to process the trauma and heal. Their lives are often clouded by a wide-range of emotional and health problems including but not limited to: depression, anxiety, suicidal thoughts, drug and alcohol abuse, and post-traumatic stress disorder. A study by the CDC called Adverse Childhood Experiences Survey (ACES) actually quantifies an ACE score through a survey to related chronic illnesses in adulthood.[22] The ACES findings suggest that certain experiences are major risk factors for the leading causes of illness and death.

The ACE score is used to assess the degree of stress experienced during childhood, and has demonstrated that as the score of the ACE survey increases, the risk for the following health problems also increases in a strong and graded fashion:

- Alcoholism and alcohol abuse
- Chronic obstructive pulmonary disease (COPD)
- Depression
- Fetal death
- Health-related quality of life
- Illicit drug use
- Ischemic heart disease (IHD)
- Liver disease
- Risk for intimate partner violence
- Multiple sexual partners
- Sexually transmitted diseases (STDs)
- Smoking
- Suicide attempts
- Unintended pregnancies
- Early initiation of smoking
- Early initiation of sexual activity
- Adolescent pregnancy

---

21 Lynne Namka, Ed. D. Shame: The Disowned Part of the Self. (1997) Talk, Trust and Feel Therapeutics. Accessed May 26, 2014. http://www.angriesout.com/teach8.htm
22 Centers for Disease Control & Prevention. http://www.cdc.gov/violenceprevention/acestudy/

As you review this list, please know that we are well aware this may be the first time you have connected your childhood trauma to mental or health problems you may have experienced over the course of your life. CSA has been declared a public health issue for at least two decades or more. Take a look at the following statement from the Centers for Disease Control dated August 29, 1997.

"CDC and the World Health Organization have declared violence prevention a public health priority (1,2). One particular form of violent victimization, child sexual abuse, is a risk factor for suicide attempts, depression, sexually transmitted diseases, and subsequent sexual assault (3). The public health approaches to child sexual abuse are intervention (e.g., treatment) and prevention. To assist in developing public health measures for preventing child sexual abuse in Vermont, in September 1995, STOP IT NOW! and Market Street Research, Inc., surveyed a representative sample of households in Vermont to assess knowledge and attitudes about child sexual abuse as a public health problem. This report summarizes the survey findings, which indicate that levels of awareness of child sexual abuse are high among Vermont residents."[23]

The trauma of CSA, including emotional pain, can indeed contribute to physical and mental health.

Are you now able to see the correlation between your health issues, physical, mental and spiritual, with the trauma of CSA? If so, in what way? _____

_____

What are some illnesses or problems you have experienced? _____

_____

Have you sought help? Has it helped? _____

_____

---

[23] Centers for Disease Control and Prevention. September 1997. Perceptions of Child Sexual Abuse as a Public Health Problem http://www.cdc.gov/mmwr/preview/mmwrhtml/00049151.htm

If you ask a survivor of child sexual abuse to identify their most prevailing emotion, the majority will name the feeling of overwhelming shame. Guilt and shame often go hand in hand. Guilt is a painful emotion characterized by having done something dishonorable, unworthy, degrading, humiliating or disgraceful. Shame internalizes guilt and says, "I am dirty, dishonorable, unworthy, degrading, humiliating or disgraceful." This feeling of shame focuses on regret, often internally tormenting us long after the abuse has ended. We all regret that we had to endure such a violation, and we all wish we had done or said something different. We may even feel shame in assuming we could have stopped the abuse. The "what if?" and the "why me?" questions torment us, considering we could have changed the course of our history. Survivors of child sexual abuse feel as though they have done something wrong, but in reality we (children) did nothing wrong. Shame is destructive emotionally and debilitating physically. We often filter our world and relationships through a position of feeling less than acceptable or devalued. From this perspective, it is impossible to be our true self, to embrace confidence and maintain a positive attitude. Have you ever been around someone who considered the glass is half empty? How about the person who predicts doom and gloom?

Do you exhibit a more positive or negative attitude? _____

What is your greatest fear? _____
_____
_____

Shame is often the road block to peace and keeps victims hiding the abuse and its secrets.

This keeps victims isolated, lonely and consumed by feelings of guilt for what happened to them. As we see from the ACES research, the trauma of childhood abuse can make you physically sick. Ironically, one of the most powerful answers to dealing with overwhelming shame is to talk about these self-destructive and toxic beliefs with a trustworthy person. The humiliation survivors feel from their abuse often makes sharing the experience impossible. Please consider the fear that surrounds sharing your abuse.

Describe how you feel about your abuse. _____
_____
_____
_____
_____
_____

Describe how you feel about yourself. _____

Reframe any toxic beliefs with positive affirmations. For example:
What I did was disgraceful. What was done to me was disgraceful.

_____
_____
_____
_____
_____
_____
_____

SHAME BASED IDENTITY

SHATTERING THE SHAME: KRISTIN'S STORY

My name is Kristin and I am a survivor of child sexual abuse from age five and continuing until the age of eleven. I was abused by a friend from school and a friend from my church. I am also dealing with a recent revelation that a friend of my family also abused me. These events shaped my life in many ways.

Shame entered my life when I was a teenager. I became intensely ashamed of my body. I would often hide my body by wearing baggy sweaters and turtlenecks and rarely swam out of fear that my body would be exposed. I hated my legs and would avoid wearing shorts, even in the summer. Because of my trauma, I didn't develop an awareness of my body as a woman and I would often dress like a teenager, even in my mid-to-late twenties. I am now in my thirties and have not yet had an intimate relationship with someone. I am still a virgin and have a hard time being alone with men. Shame has also impacted my self-esteem. I've felt responsible about the things that were done to me as a child, even though I now realize they weren't my fault. There were people that I hurt in the midst of being abused and I struggled with shame from that.

After telling my parents about my abuse, they yelled at me and caused further secondary trauma. They silenced my voice, and in turn I felt ashamed about what I had done and who I was. I struggled with self-confidence and being worthy of love. I have shame about what the friend of my family did to me, although I have forgiven him and I am in the process of healing from that. I still have a difficult time exposing certain parts of my body, but I am currently in the process of healing from that as well. I am learning to love my body as it is, and have been trying to see myself as God sees me. I have been able to receive a lot of healing in the past few years. I am in a much better place and am taking baby steps to overcome this issue. I pray to receive healing so that one day I can experience true intimacy as God intended it. It is the desire of my heart to marry and to have a family. With the help of God and my loving support system, I continue my journey of healing.

Kristin shared how shame has impacted her self-image, body image, self-esteem, and relationships. Not only did she blame herself for her abuse; but when she told her parents, the disclosure was met with blame, anger and denial which further fueled her feelings that she was responsible. Her response to her own self-image and identity is a common response.

Mary Ann Cohen, director of The New York Center for Eating Disorders wrote, "Sexual abuse can have many different effects on the eating habits and body image of survivors. Sexual abuse violates the boundaries of the self so dramatically that inner sensations of hunger, fatigue, or sexuality become difficult to identify. People who have been sexually abused may turn to food to relieve a wide range of different states of tension that have nothing to do with hunger. It is their confusion and uncertainty about their inner perceptions that leads them to focus on the food."[24]

Many survivors of sexual abuse often work to become very fat or very thin in an attempt to render themselves unattractive. In this way, they try to de-sexualize themselves. Other survivors obsessively diet, starve, or purge to make their bodies "perfect." A perfect body is their attempt to feel more powerful, invulnerable, and in control, so as not to re-experience the powerlessness they felt as abused children.[25] Indeed, some large men and women, who are survivors of sexual abuse, are afraid to lose weight because it will render them feeling small and childlike. This, in turn, may bring back painful memories with which to cope.

There is mounting evidence that problems occur when shame or humiliation becomes an integral part of a person's self-image or sense of self-worth. Over the past two decades, psychologists, psychiatrists and other mental health professionals have reported that abnormal methods of handling shame play an important role in social phobias, eating disorders, domestic violence, substance abuse, road-rage, schoolyard and workplace rampages, sexual offenses and a host of other personal and social problems. Dr. Marilyn J. Sorensen, a clinical psychologist and author of *Breaking the Chain of Low Self-Esteem*, explains how such disorders originate with the following statement:

---

24   Mary Ann Cohen. This article is adapted from her book, *French Toast for Breakfast: Declaring Peace with Emotional Eating* and published on the website, Eating Disorder Referral and Information Center, International Eating Disorder Referral Organization. Accessed May 27, 2014 from http://www.edreferral.com/sexual_abuse_&_ed.htm
25   Child Abuse & Neglect, Volume 19, Issue 12, December 1995, Pages 1401–1421

"Early in life, individuals develop an internalized view of themselves as adequate or inadequate within the world. Children who are continually criticized, severely punished, neglected, abandoned, or in other ways abused or mistreated get the message that they do not 'fit' in the world; that they are inadequate, inferior or unworthy."[26]

These feelings of inferiority are the genesis of low self-esteem, Sorenson says. Individuals with low self-esteem become overly sensitive and fearful in many situations. They are afraid they won't know the rules or that they've blundered, misspoken or acted in ways others might consider inappropriate. Or, they might perceive that others reject or are critical of them.[27]

Once low self-esteem is formed, a person becomes hypersensitive. They experience "self-esteem attacks" that take the form of embarrassment or shame, Sorenson adds. Unlike guilt, which is the feeling of doing something wrong, shame is the feeling of *being* something wrong. When a person experiences shame, they feel "there is something basically wrong with me."[28]

Aaron Kipnis, Ph.D., author of *Angry Young Men: How Parents, Teachers and Counselors Can Help Bad Boys Become Good Men* and a clinical psychologist in private practice in Santa Barbara, California, agrees. He says shame's effects are more damaging than those of guilt.

"Guilt is positive. It's a response of psychologically healthy individuals who realize they have done something wrong. It helps them act more positively, more responsibly, often to correct what they've done. But shame is not productive. Shame tends to direct individuals into destructive behaviors. When we focus on what we did wrong, we can correct it; but when we're convinced we are wrong as a result of shame, our whole sense of self is eroded. That's why guilt doesn't produce the anger, rage or other irrational behaviors shame does. Many violent behaviors lead back to a deep well of shame."[29]

---

26 Holly Vanscoy. (2006). Shame: The Quintessential Emotion. Psych Central. Retrieved on May 27, 2014, from http://psychcentral.com/lib/shame-the-quintessential-emotion/000730
27 Ibid.
28 Ibid.
29 Ibid.

Let's take a closer look at behaviors characterized by shame:[30]

- Feeling "something is wrong with me" – everything is colored by shame
- Fear of rejection is very strong
- Isolated and lonely – fearful when someone wants to have a close relationship
- Fearful of intimacy – wanting relationship but pushing people away
- Defensive when criticized
- Entering into people-pleasing behavior patterns – not aware of how to get own needs met

- Punishing self with negative and destructive self-talk – or physical harm
- Feeling over-responsible for everyone and everything that happens
- Aggressive or abusive behavior
- Having problems with depression

Realizing behaviors linked to shame-based thinking and the impact shame has had in our lives is often the first step in making the necessary behavior changes to live a healthier lifestyle.

Can you identify any shame-based behaviors from this list that you may currently have or have struggled with in the past? _____
_____
_____

Is there someone in your life who wants to get close to you and because of your filter of abuse you have kept him or her at bay? _____
_____
_____

---

30 Source: Adapted and put into by own words from an idea in "Helping Victims of Sexual Abuse"– Heitritter and Vought – Bethany House Publishers – Published 1989)

BLAME OF SHAME

SHATTERING THE SHAME: ANGELA'S STORY

For 14 years I suffered physical, verbal, emotional and sexual abuse by my stepfather with many tears but without one scream. For many of those years when summoned, I made the long walk to the back bedroom where the bedspread would be neatly folded back from the foot of the bed, and I took my position for the 30 minutes of his evil pleasure and then got up, feeling nauseous, proceeded to the bathroom and clawed my face, trying to peel off the wax of shame.

Because Angela had been sexually abused for so many years and kept silent, she felt powerless and was manipulated to believe the sex act was consensual. We suffer with so much confusion because in our compliancy we feel consensual in the act of sexual abuse and nothing is farther from the truth. The compliant victimization (the term compliant in no way means consensual) is the most difficult concept for people to accept and understand. Shame smothers those of us who feel somehow we were consensual in the act of abuse. Not only do we heap shame on ourselves, but also do those well-meaning people in our lives who ask, "Why didn't you tell? Why didn't you scream?" or "Why did you let it go on for so long?" Though these questions are honest, they do not realize for a second how these words cut deep. They don't realize how these questions heap boulders of blame and suggest consent implying we had some power and control over the abuse. Furthermore, those are redundant questions we have asked ourselves: "Why didn't I tell, scream, and run?" We torment ourselves with these questions. Most people do not understand the immense power and control, fear and intimidation a perpetrator wields. They also do not understand the warped dynamic of the abusive relationship. In the majority of child sexual abuse cases, 93% of the time we know, we trust and even love the person who is abusing us. The relationship continues outside of the abuse in social settings. There is an enormous emotional dichotomy. We have a personal emotional investment in the life of our abuser, as do those closest to us.

Child grooming comprises actions by a perpetrator deliberately undertaken with the aim of befriending and establishing an emotional connection with a child, to lower the child's inhibitions in order to sexually abuse the child. This same grooming takes place with the caregiver in a child's life. This is why we so often hear, "He is just not capable of doing such a horrific act." We as a society are looking for the monster among us as the face of an abuser. We must alter this assumption. Abusers are woven into every fabric of our society, every profession, every ethnic group, every socio-economic status, and may be as close as a parent. The abuser may act decisively and quickly or may groom potential victims over months breaking down barriers of resistance. The abuse may happen once or over the course of many years. In any case, the abuse is always a violent and heinous act. As survivors we rationalize the severity of our attacks. We may think, it really wasn't that bad because there was no penetration. Many survivors minimize the abuse, and lack the validation from society based on its severity. When our innocence was violently taken we can never have it restored. If it happened for 10 seconds or 10 years, the abuse still impacts our lives. Instead of accepting the harm done to us, many may feel responsible for the act, the consequences perpetrators receive, and the damage done to their reputation, if their egregious behavior is exposed. When a family member is involved, we are charged with protecting the family's reputation by keeping the "loved one" from incarceration. In most cases, we are encouraged to stay silent for the good of the family, and excuses are made for the behavior. This lack of support forces us to take on the dysfunctional and cowardly behavior mirrored in the family. What few realize is the internal war this causes: desperately wanting justice, fearful that the abuser will sexually assault other children, yet bound to silence by those we love the most. It is rare a survivor of child sexual abuse as a child or an adult will seek justice alone. What most of society does not accept is that child sexual abuse is a crime, and by covering up this crime, society is actually an accomplice. Like rape, child molestation is one of the most underreported crimes. Only 1-10% of cases of child sexual abuse are ever disclosed. (Source: FBI Law Enforcement Bulletin.) To make matters worse, in most cases justice is rare in our court system. Forensic evidence is difficult to preserve, thus sex offenders rarely receive any punishment and continue on their abusive rampage. On average, a sex offender has 117 victims in his or her lifetime.

A battle rages between wanting justice but grappling and feeling responsible for sending grandpa, aunt, uncle or brother to jail. The family often turns on the accuser, and many survivors report being treated as a traitor or an outcast. Collateral damage is always a consequence to child sexual abuse resulting in the proverbial white elephant at every family reunion, holiday gathering and birthday party.

Children cannot give consent; it is against the law of nature and the land. Consent implies that an individual is of age and wants to engage in sexual behavior versus the reality of that child being groomed, manipulated, and overpowered into sexual activity. Yet in our courtrooms today this defense is used: "The child seduced me."

In a court case in Montana, a 14-year-old girl was sexually abused by her teacher. The instructor was found guilty and sentenced to 30 days in jail because the judge said, "She does not look 14." Tragically, the 14-year-old took her life after hearing the sentence. This precious child had the courage to tell and was let down by the system.

Abusers deliver confusing messages in an attempt to keep their victim silenced. "This is our secret, no one must know," or "I know you like it," or "You will get in so much trouble if you tell," or "I will kill your (fill in the blank)," or worse yet, "If you tell no one will believe you." Then there are the threats of harm to those you love which creates paralyzing fear. When a victim believes the physical threats leveraged against a mother or a younger sibling, that threat becomes a heavy burden for the child to bear, another's safety their burden. In order to protect loved ones, we become a compliant victim. Abuse typically occurs within a long-term, on-going relationship between the offender and victim, escalates over time and lasts an average of four years. Cases have been reported that have lasted much longer.

So, as adults how do we reconcile this shame from feeling consensual in the act of child sexual abuse? We understand that as a child we had no power and no voice; we acknowledge that our act of compliance and obedience in the face of confusion and fear is just exactly how we were trained as children to respond; we are taught early on to obey authority, trust friends and family and to never question affectionate advances. We must start to be free of the shame that causes so much mental distress by putting the shame back on the abuser.

As survivors of child sexual abuse, we often look back at the situation as adults and feel we could have or should have done something differently to prevent our victimization. We must accept that we had very little power. We imagine the choices we had as children are the same as the ones available now as adults. Not so. Survivors make certain choices they feel are in their best interest at the time of their abuse.

They later can feel (and this is often inferred by the abuser as well) that their choices somehow indicated collusion in the abuse. This misconception intensifies the shame and mental trauma. In order to start feeling free from this mental manipulation, it is critical to understand that abuse is largely about power and intention on the abuser's part.

EXERCISE:

Drive to a park and observe children playing. Notice their vulnerability and gullibility. Do you feel any of those children have the mental or physical power to protect themselves?

_____
_____
_____
_____
_____

SHAME OF PHYSICAL RESPONSE

SHATTERING THE SHAME: ANGELA'S STORY

I didn't stop the abuse. I didn't scream. I didn't say no. Sometimes I didn't even cry. So does that equal consent? Even more shameful was the fact that I could not control the primal instincts to respond. I was forced into silence by threats that my stepfather would kill my mother if I told. I did not question his threats as I witnessed severe abuse that left me paralyzed in fear. The toxic tar of shame spread through my mind like a flesh-eating bacteria: eating away at any self-worth, self-respect, self-dignity, self-power and eventually making me view myself as evil, dark and as perverse as my abuser. I hated every time he touched me, yet I could not stop my body from responding.

Angela carried a tremendous amount of shame from feeling as though she was participating in the sexual act. This is a very common reaction among survivors of sexual abuse whose bodies seemed to betray them and responded to the abuse.

While Dr. Brian Kassar wrote this statement concerning adult males, it is understood by therapists and counselors to apply to children as well. He wrote: "It is a myth that men who get an erection or ejaculate during a sexual assault gave consent or enjoyed the assault. Erection and ejaculation are physiological responses that can't be controlled and can even result from stress. These responses can be confusing for a man who has been sexually assaulted and can make him wonder if he really did enjoy or want the sexual contact. An erection or ejaculation does not equal consent."[31]

Survivors are encouraged to realize that they were powerless in the midst of their abuse. They must also understand they have no way of controlling the physiological responses of their bodies, even in the midst of such a heinous crime.

---

31 Santa Clara University. (2002). - The Wellness Center. Retrieved June 6, 2014, from http://www.scu.edu/wellness/topics/family/malesexabuse.cfm

You see, children are staunchly taught to respect adult authority, even punished for a hint of disrespect. They have a narrow view of what you are allowed to refuse from an adult or older youth. To some extent we are born stripped of the ability and personal power to protect ourselves. We look for adult models to teach us right from wrong, and we are confused when we learn wrong for right. Abusers manipulatively teach their victims that inappropriate sex is their way of showing affection. Some children are starved for affirmation and attention, which makes children easy prey. The shame thickens when we cannot control primal responses. We are even more mortified when that response is rubbed in our face by our abusers.

Sadly, we have experienced the worst of humanity when considering abusers acting out their perversion on helpless beings. Predators further convince us we have the same sexual desire as they do and the sex act is consensual to ease their own conscience. Some victimizers even cause us such tremendous fear through intimidation or physical abuse that we do not question their evil threats.

This dynamic is so complex that in some cases we even want to protect our abusers, or protect those who will be pained by our disclosure. We even attempt to please our abusers in a warped relationship that says, "I will get in trouble if anyone knows what I have done or even worse, the shame of someone finding out I had sexual relations with my own (father, pastor, sister, brother, aunt, etc.)." We are so terrified of what will happen to our abusers, what they will do to us, what others will say, do or feel about us if they find out that it almost seems counterproductive to spill the beans. As painful as suffering in silence is for many survivors, it often seems the only option in a maze of "what ifs."

Another layer of shame is heaped on victims when those charged to protect them deny the disclosure. Immediately, when we are not believed we are given the message that we do not matter, our abuser is worthy of protection, we caused the abuse and there is no one to protect us.

EXERCISE:

Find a picture of yourself at the time of the abuse, put the photo in a chair and tell your inner child you love her and you forgive her for not having the ability to refuse, reject the physical response, or tell, scream or run.

Release the rage against your abuser, those charged to protect you and all those who denied your abuse. Scream, yell or hit a pillow.

Identify behaviors in your life that create continued feelings of shame. _____
_____
_____
_____

MASKING THE SHAME

SHATTERING THE SHAME: POLLY'S STORY

One of my first memories of being sexually abused was when I was about eight years old and I was told to come inside a neighbor's house. There were two brothers who were the same age and friends with my older brothers. I don't remember what exact threats were made to make me stay and not run away, but soon I was forcefully performing oral sex on one brother and then the other. At this young age I had no idea what was happening to me, but my first steps outside their front door after it was finally over was instantly shaking under the weight of the shame that I truly believed would be forever part of me.

As I grew older I could only describe my shame as becoming a clear Plexiglas wall that was always parallel – right in front of me. Wherever I went, it followed in every direction like an unseen shadow that was forever part of me. I could never see the wall because I had never experienced life without it. In each stage of my life, my old secret developed new layers of shame, becoming stronger with each new layer and forever separating me from the world. Through it I could see everyone and everyone could see me. I watched the world and they watched me, but we were never to meet. I was sexually abused from the age of eight to the age of twelve and my testimony falls into the category of the 1 in 10 that never tell. After 40 years of silence, my wall of shame became thicker as each year put on another layer of shame, and now had me convinced that I would never break though the growing thickness of shame.

Sadly, Polly lived her life with a mask that separated her from the world. She lived in a world in which she felt like a spectator and not a participant. Shame makes us want to HIDE our "real" self from others and could result in suffering:

▸ Behaving in a dissociative manner.

▸ Abandoning our true identity (reinventing ourselves)

▸ Bearing a heavy burden of everyone's dysfunction

▸ Seeking "normal" and thinking everything is our fault

▸ Distorting boundaries

Justin and Lindsay Holcomb in their new book, *Rid of My Disgrace*, comment on shame this way, "Perhaps the greatest fear of a person marked by shameful defilement is the fear of exposure. Consequently, they often labor to present themselves to others in the way that they wish they were instead of being honest about their brokenness and need."[32]

---

[32] Justin S. Holcomb and Lindsey A. Holcomb. *Rid of My Disgrace: Hope and Healing for Victims of Sexual Assault*. Crossway: January 5, 2011.

Shame can cause a host of toxic beliefs or emotions such as:

Hatred	Humiliation	Illegitimacy
Occult Involvement	Self-Accusation	Self-Hate
Self-Pity	Shunning	Guilt
Inferiority	Abandonment	Anger
Bad Boy/Girl	Being Different	Condemnation
Defilement	Disgrace	Embarrassment

There is a huge commitment that we must make in altering such toxic beliefs and feelings to retrain our brain and take these toxic beliefs captive in an effort to live a healthier and happier life. **We must begin to commit to love and value ourselves.** If we respect and value ourselves, we encourage others to respect and value us. If you abuse yourself or allow others to do so, you tell others that abusive behavior is okay with you.

The bottom line is that we must peel off those masks and learn to love our true selves so others can love us. We must be firm in building healthy boundaries and encourage healthy relationships and remove unhealthy relationships from our lives. Additionally, if you are engaging in activity or behavior that is causing even more shame in your life, it is time to radically change that behavior. Perhaps because of child sexual abuse trauma you have a sexual addiction and you are struggling with a pornography addiction in isolation. You are creating layers of shame in your life that you need help to recover.

Have you experienced any of the above toxic behaviors, beliefs or emotions? _____
_____
Can you share one goal in taking a step toward your recovery? _____
_____
_____

THE SHAME OF FEELING UNCLEAN

SHATTERING THE SHAME: ANGELA'S STORY

The shame made me feel dirty. I would scald myself with steaming baths to try and melt the wax of shame and feel clean. I would take scalding showers to feel clean, but as soon as I turned to the mirror I saw a toxic message that screamed "you are not clean!"

I have spent the past 31 years trying to really live, after grappling with just wanting to die, taking 64 sleeping pills with vodka. I've spent many days trying to peel the shame away to figure out the why? I will never know the why. Today there are still slivers of the wax of shame coating that I continue to peel away on the journey of healing. I don't feel the coat that disguised my identify, just residue from time to time.

Angela could not feel clean, even after scalding baths. Sexual abuse is a degrading, humiliating violation that robs the human spirit of power, pride, confidence and self-worth. How do we shatter the shame and begin the long process to healing? One step at a time, one layer at a time.

In the words of one of our contemporary scholars of identifying shame, Gershen Kaufman: "Shame is the most disturbing experience individuals ever have about themselves; no other emotion feels more deeply disturbing because in the moment of shame the self feels wounded from within."[33]

Angela felt unclean internally, and scalding showers were not the answer. Shame is the FEELING and the thoughts that we are somehow wrong, defective, inadequate, not good enough, or not strong enough. While everyone feels shame, most of us do not recognize it in its many forms. We can experience fleeting shame at burping loudly in an elevator. Or we

---

33 Jane Bolton. What We Get Wrong About Shame: Why is shame such a powerful emotion. Psychology Today. Accessed June 6, 2014 from http://www.psychologytoday.com/blog/your-zesty-self/200905/what-we-get-wrong-about-shame

can feel chronic shame, experiencing that we, as a whole person, are flawed and inferior. We can feel different intensities of shame. The most intense is humiliation. Humiliation is so painful that we can think, "This is so painful I wish I could just die!" This is the most pervasive level of shame experienced by survivors of child sexual abuse.

Suicidal thoughts and beliefs are a real struggle. We just want the pain to end and we feel as though ending our life is the only solution. These very disturbing thoughts of suicide and self-harm must be shared and cannot be conquered in isolation. If you experience suicidal thoughts, please seek professional help. The shame of child sexual abuse robs us of our ability to see the world clearly and accept pure unadulterated love. Know that you are a person with unique gifts and talents.

Have you experienced suicidal thoughts? _____

Have you ever attempted suicide? _____

What is your plan to get help if you are struggling with suicidal thoughts? _____
_____
_____

SHAME SOLUTIONS

To help relieve shame in your own mind (or the person you are supporting), it is important to understand right from the start of the abuse, that the child is not to blame; and the abuser had malicious intent. It is vital to remember that even though there may have been an exchange of money or favors, this is not consent. Perpetrators will use anything at their disposal to bribe a child with sweets, affection or money. But as a child or young person, sexual involvement or gratification was never that child's *original intent in the relationship.* Some questions for consideration:

- Critically – who had the real power in that situation?
- Who originally initiated the inappropriate abusive acts?
- What was your fundamental motive as a child when you met this person?
- What was the abuser's primary motive?
- Who was leading?
- Who was being led?
- Did you do things just to "get it over with"?
- If this person gave you affection, did you get much attention elsewhere in your life?
- If you accepted favorable treatment, sweets or money, did you really understand what was happening?
- If you could have told someone, who realistically would have helped you?
- Did you exhibit behaviors that something was wrong and no one intervened?
- Were you threatened or was someone you care about threatened with harm?
- If your abuse was a brutal attack, did you have the physical power to defend yourself?

It is important to note that, even if your answers do not make you feel absolved of shame, abuse can make you feel things and act in ways alien to you. This does not make you responsible for another's actions or change who you really are. Nor does it diminish the severity of the crime perpetrated against you.

It is critical to understand that abuse and shame exist in an environment of secrecy and the way out of shame (including any shame) is to **talk about it.** Sharing these "secrets" in a trustworthy, supportive environment frees you of the burden to carry it alone. It helps put the shame back on the correct person – the abuser – so the journey of mental and emotional recovery can really begin. This sharing could be in a recovery group, with a counselor, through close friends or a combination of these.

Ellen Bass and Laura David wrote a breakthrough book called *Courage to Heal* and beautifully capture how powerful breaking free from shame and silence can be: "Shame exists in an environment of secrecy. When you begin to freely speak the truth about your life, your sense of shame will diminish. Secrets destroy people and they destroy them unnecessarily. It's like being reborn when you shed the secret, because you have no more fear". (Source: *Courage To Heal* by Ellen Bass and Laura David – Cedar 1988 page 108)

Freeing yourself from shame can be a long arduous process. Isolating yourself can be a natural response to so much pain; however, loneliness can bring even more suffering. Time after time survivors of abuse say that just speaking out to a counselor or being in a support group with other survivors has helped tremendously. This might not be right for you, but do consider joining a self-help group or community group that can provide the companions you need in your journey toward recovery.

In reviewing the previous questions, was there one individual who particularly helped you to remove the shame from yourself and place it on your abuser? Explain.

_____
_____
_____

OVERCOMING SHAME-BASED THINKING

Many of our feelings are simple reactions to specific events that we perceive as pleasant or unpleasant. After the event is over, the related feeling usually fades away. We can easily see that our emotions are fleeting and impermanent.

Shame does not work this way. The hallmark of shame is a constant awareness of our defects. Without realizing it, we become continual victims of shame-based thinking. Every day, we focus on our failures. Every day, we re-convince ourselves that we are defective. Our thoughts become riddled with judgment, regret, and images of impending failure.

When we consciously articulate these shame-based thoughts, we might be shocked at their severity. In *Letting Go of Shame*, Ronald Potter-Efron and Patricia Potter-Efron[34] list the following examples.

- I am defective (damaged, broken, a mistake, flawed).
- I am dirty (soiled, ugly, unclean, impure, filthy, disgusting).
- I am incompetent (not good enough, inept, ineffectual, useless).
- I am unwanted (unloved, unappreciated, uncherished).
- I am weak (small, impotent, puny, feeble).
- I am bad (awful, dreadful, evil, despicable).
- I am pitiful (contemptible, miserable, insignificant).
- I am nothing (worthless, invisible, unnoticed, empty).

Which one of these statements best describes your struggle with shame? _____
_____
_____

Take each statement and rephrase it to a more positive and healthy belief about yourself. _____
_____
_____

---

34 Passage on shame-based thoughts cited from Ronald Potter-Efron and Patricia Potter-Efron's *Letting Go of Shame: Understanding How Shame Affects Your Life* (Center City, MN: Hazelden, 1989), 14, 115.

Shame develops as the slow, relentless accumulation of such thoughts: one self-insult at a time, delivered to ourselves over weeks, months and years. Notice that each of the previous statements starts with the words *I am*. This reinforces our definition of shame as a state of being that goes far beyond anything we do or fail to do.

If we look closely, we can see that those shame-based thoughts exist on more than one level. The first level is an exhaustive list of our faults. The second level is an added message that those faults are permanent. In short, the first level is "I am not good." The second level is, "I'll never be good enough."

In addition, it does not matter how well we perform in school, on the job, or at home. Shame-based thinking lingers and colors the way we perceive everything. It leads us to automatically discount our skills and successes. Even if we receive recognition or praise, shame-based thinking forces us to explain it away: *I don't deserve appreciation. . . . If only they knew who I really am. . . . They don't really mean what they're saying. . . . They're just setting me up for failure.*

Other Hazelden authors agree that shame-based thoughts tend to be permanent and pervasive. These authors go on to identify additional features of shame-based thinking.[35]

- Negative explanations of other people's behavior
- Dire predictions
- Selective focus on negative aspects of events
- Doubt in coping skills
- Rigid rules about how people should behave
- Unrealistic expectations about people and events

Thinking that is marked by these characteristics leads to several paradoxical results.

---

[35] Excerpted from the e-book, *How to Change Your Thinking About Shame: A Hazelden Quick Guide.* Published by Hazelden, 2012. Visit the Hazelden bookstore for more information.

First: we often believe we are responsible, when the truth is we are just attempting to control our circumstances. This results from our rigid rules for how other people should behave and for how events should unfold. Trying to enforce those rules leads us to monitor other people's behavior and criticize them whenever they violate one of our many expectations.

Second: we become prey for perfectionism. Only an error-free performance can ever satisfy the demands imposed by shame-based thinking. Mistakes are disasters and cannot be openly admitted. The paradox is that we cling to perfection while remaining constantly aware of our imperfections.

Third: being highly critical of ourselves makes us highly critical of other people. We see our own faults mirrored in our family members, friends, and co-workers. We judge them, and in turn they perceive us as arrogant and self-righteous. The truth is that we see little of value in ourselves.

Fourth: a final paradox is that we see our self-defeating thoughts as a form of self-protection and a way to escape from shame. In reality, we find ourselves even more victimized by shame than ever. We continually focus on the worst that could possibly happen: every new project resulting in failure, every new relationship ending in pain. In our mind, we relive mistakes over and over again, trying to explain and understand them, hoping to prevent them from ever happening again. In the end, we just feel more sad and fearful. Our shame is reinforced.

What shame-based thinking can you identify? _____

Share the last memory of a situation that involved shame-based thinking interaction and how the other person responded. _____
_____
_____
_____

CHALLENGE SHAME-BASED THOUGHTS

There's a saying, "Don't believe everything you think." This is a core principle of cognitive-behavioral therapy. Instead of viewing your thoughts as absolute truths, see them as mental events to observe and evaluate. Be willing to challenge shame-based thoughts and replace them with more accurate thoughts.

As explained earlier, shame-based thinking has several characteristics. It is often based on dire predictions, doubt in your coping skills, selective focus on negative aspects of events, negative explanations of others' behavior, and rigid rules about how people should behave.

Choose a specific thought you would like to work with, such as *I'll never find a job* or, *if this relationship ends, I'll never get over it, I'll never be a good wife, mother, or friend*. Then challenge this thought by asking any of the following questions:

- Is this thought really true?
- How do I know it is true?
- What is the evidence for this thought?
- What is the evidence against this thought?
- Can I think of any times when this thought has not been true?
- Is this thought helping me or hurting me?
- Who would I be if I let go of this thought?
- What could I do if I let go of this thought?
- Am I willing to release this thought?
- What is the worst that could happen if I let go of this thought? Can I live with that?

Which shame-based thinking can you identify in the last section? _____
_____
_____

What challenge question can you apply to this shame-based thought? _____
_____
_____

COLLATERAL DAMAGE

SHATTERING THE SHAME: JIMMY'S STORY

Words cannot adequately describe the shame and stigma attached to families of pedophiles. Dad was sentenced the same week of the Sandusky trial, so there was a national spotlight on sex offenders at the time. It was tough enough experiencing the public shame and humiliation the newspapers and local news channels subjected the entire family to. But then came the letters to the editor, wishing dad to be raped in prison. The same week it hit the news, I received a call from dad's appalled landlord telling me to have all of his stuff out in two days. The trauma seemed likely to never end, and three years later we still are trying to wrap our minds around the reality of it all. Within minutes, the father we all grew up knowing, respecting, and loving had a dark secret double life that was now exposed to the world.

My dad will die in prison. Make no mistake, he worked very hard to earn that sentence, and I believe the sentence is just. However, as strange as it may sound, he is still our father. At some point ten siblings, our mother, and I will have to make decisions on whether or not to hold a memorial service. I am the minister of the family (following in dad's footsteps), so most eyes will look to me for guidance. Most of the family has not had any correspondence with dad for almost three years. Perhaps they're holding on to their last positive encounter with him. The effects of abuse move far beyond the victims. I'm preaching at the same church my dad preached at for 27 years of his life. I was the one who turned my father in to the police. And, I was the one who had to stand before the church, who loved and respected my father, and tell them that he was being arrested for child molestation. I had to find a way to gracefully answer the questions every church member had on their mind: "Was my child one of his victims?"

In spite of the shame and stigma associated with dad's crimes, we are not defined by it. It's easier to overcome shame when you don't allow it to define you. Victims begin to heal when they shed the lie that the abuse was somehow their fault. I've realized that it's so vital to take a strong stand against abuse and let survivors know that their past abuse does not define who they are now. We may wear shame as an unwelcome garment for a time, but over time we can help each other shed it piece by piece until it is gone.

We are so laser focused on our own pain that we often forget that the tentacles of shame and disappointment reach far into the lives of families associated with the abuse. We see from Jimmy's account, a son whose foundation was rocked when his father's criminal behavior of sexual abuse was exposed. As survivors we see from our single-focus lens and may not consider how those in our lives and the lives of our abusers have also been impacted. Jimmy had great words of advice: "It is easier to overcome shame when you don't let it define you." He shares wise counsel, that we need each other to help shed the shame by speaking out against child sexual abuse. In contrast to Jimmy's story, there are those in our life who reject our disclosure and do not believe our abuse to be true, and that could cause further shame. Compassion and forgiveness for them is our own journey to healing.

Is there someone in your abuser's life to whom you might need to extend compassion for the shame they are carrying because of their actions? _____

_____
_____

A MOTHER'S SHAME

SHATTERING THE SHAME: CYNDI'S STORY

"I felt someone put their hands in my pants." Those are the words I heard from my then 10-year-old daughter one morning. We later got a confession from my father-in-law. I had a flood of emotions running through me that moment; heck, that whole day. One of them was guilt; guilt that I didn't protect her. Guilt that I didn't know he was capable of molesting his own granddaughter. For a while, I felt guilty for even sharing our story, thinking that WE had something to be ashamed of.

My guilt eventually turned to anger, resentment, bitterness, and even hatred toward this man I once called "dad." I couldn't go a day without spewing some form of hatred towards him, whether in conversation with someone else, or an angry entry in my journal. Through counseling, a recovery program, and eventually being able to tell our story out loud to an audience, I found some healing, freedom, and peace. I learned to forgive and what that REALLY looks like. I no longer feel any shame or guilt. My way of parenting will never be the same. I will ALWAYS look extra close at someone and their intentions, but I also no longer live in fear. I'm probably more educated on this subject than my own parents ever were, but that's a good thing. Education and standing up for yourself and those who cannot do so on their own will bring a level of strength to everyone involved.

We still deal with a roller coaster of emotions from time to time, but we are never ashamed to tell our story. **Revelations 12:11** *says, "They triumphed over him by the blood of the Lamb and by the word of their testimony."*

Unfortunately, some mothers look the other way and are in deep denial over the sexual abuse of their children, especially if the abuser is a husband or boyfriend. When mothers who fiercely protect their children receive a disclosure of sexual abuse, their road to healing is often arduous, riddled with emotions of guilt, anger and shame. In Cyndi's story, and most stories, there is an enormous amount of guilt over not protecting her child and not realizing the dangers that loomed so close. At Angela's Voice we are vigilant in teaching that every child is at risk, and you cannot identify a perpetrator in a crowd. We sometimes believe we have radar that allows us to identify abusers by a disfiguring mark like a monster so we can confidently say, "Yes, there is the risk for my child." Not so. As Cyndi shared, she was not aware her father-in-law was capable of such an act. She was not aware of the history of sexual abuse that had been hidden for years. If the first accusations in this family had been addressed responsibly, perhaps Cyndi's child could have been saved this trauma. The healing from sexual abuse in a family is the responsibility of every member involved. Trust has been destroyed and the judgment of others is another root of shame. Once again we see that breaking the silence and sharing the pain and shame is a path to healing.

If you are a parent of a survivor, how have you dealt with your child's abuse? If you are a survivor, how have your parents dealt with your sexual abuse? _____
_____
_____

FAITH AS A TOOL TO OVERCOME SHAME

SHATTERING THE SHAME: JO ANN'S STORY

I spent my first forty years in failed relationships and lost count of the heartbreaks. Healthy, intimate connections required trust, and my father had stolen that many years ago. The pain rooted deep, shaping me into a woman of low self-worth, leaving me voiceless for decades. For years, silence stood as my willing guardian, shielding me from the fallout of sexual abuse and the shame of revealing family secrets. I walked most of my days with this pressing fear of being "found out." Shame suppresses the heart, making one mute. Maybe it has happened to you? Maybe you've been shamed or intimidated into silence? And over time, maybe you've adopted the voice of an imposter? You know the one, the "life-is-just-fine, thanks-for-asking" mask. Daily you reach for it and hide behind it, while you live a life on the outside that is deeply divorced from your innermost truth. Maybe you have buried your true self in family, career, and service to others, pretending immunity from any past or present emotional wounds?

Perhaps you're tempted by the thoughts even now. Keep it in check. No one can know. No one will understand – they may even blame me.

It doesn't have to be this way. Over time, in the shadow of Jesus, I addressed my unhealthy belief system. As I applied the truth of scripture to negative emotional thought patterns, I learned to think new thoughts about old experiences, to "retrain" my brain. Healing begins at truth-telling. We cannot change anything about our lives without first knowing and facing the truth. When we confront this nothingness, this pain of silence, we release the hold it has on us. Shame, humiliation, or fear cannot withstand the piercing light of Truth.

There is an extraordinary power in telling the truth to someone who validates you by simply listening. In this safe place, honor somehow washes away the stench of shame. I get it: how after we've been hurt, it's hard to trust someone--anyone. It's hard to start over when someone has robbed us of our childlike natural trust. But this holding in, holding back, it hurts much worse than the pain of allowing someone else in. I've lived this and earned the right to say so.

God's not a fan of unhealthy secret-keeping. He doesn't want us hiding in shame, lying about our situation, or pretending to be someone we're not in order to be accepted or loved. Jesus made the sacrifice He did so we would live in the light of freedom. It's a terrifying yet liberating crossroads; the realization that silence, shame, guilt, or any sort of emotional torment cannot rob us of God's love, of His plans for our lives, no matter what we've walked through.

We may struggle with faith. For those who believe in God, we wonder, "Why did God let this happen?" or "Where was God in my abuse?" Others may be ashamed and think they are too damaged for God to love them. Some people will even blame God and are mad at Him for not intervening. Jo Ann has found her strength in God and in allowing Him to bring healing and comfort in a close relationship. She has been able to receive the love of God, find comfort in scripture and walking in truth. Spiritual healing is a great tool that brings serenity and peace into your life. We would be remiss if we did not address the egregious behavior of the church and the part they have played in sexual abuse. We have no excuses for the abuse that is in and around the church and in every religion, but if we are not there in the midst of, how can we play a part in battling this evil?

Where do you find your strength? _____

_____

_____

If faith plays a role in your healing, please take a few moments and search your heart for any emotions that may be blocking your relationship with God. _____

_____

_____

COMPASSION CALLS

SHATTERING THE SHAME: ANGELA'S STORY

As I stood in the mirror, I felt inches of thick wax coating of shame over my whole body. I would look in the mirror and attempt to peel the shame away, clawing at my face, feeling the pain of sharp fingernails in my flesh but knowing I would never get to the layer of innocence that was stripped away. I have had to learn to love the person in the mirror.

We hope you have received insights, hope, and encouragement through this study. Healing is a journey. Please accept that you are not to blame and you should carry no shame for the abuse you have suffered. We realize those words are often easier to hear than they are to receive. So we are going to ask that you take a few moments now to allow your inner child to release any of the blame and resulting shame from your experiences. Somewhere between hating the abuse we begin to hate ourselves. It is so difficult to give love or receive love if we do not even know how to love ourselves. The shame of sexual abuse steals our ability to love ourselves. If we encounter a wounded child today, we would have extreme

compassion. Often our disclosures of sexual abuse are coming out of the mouth of an adult and the child that was so profoundly wounded is lost in the translation. We need to offer that same compassion to our inner child that we would offer to a stranger. Just because others do not respond in a compassionate and caring way to your disclosure of abuse does not mean that you cannot treat yourself with compassion and care. In your confusion you need to resolve some issues.

Please take a field trip to a place of comfort for you, from your childhood. It may be the beach, the swings on the playground, under a favorite oak tree. When you and your inner child are on that field trip, share some truths with yourself, that perhaps you have longed to hear. Give that child what he or she so desperately longs for: compassion, nurture and a release from the blame of her sexual abuse.

SMILE

The shame of child sexual abuse has often stolen our smile and the feeling that all is right with the world. It tends to put a veil over the bright light of gleeful joy that shines in a child. We encourage you to smile again; not the pretend smile with gritted teeth, but the smile that takes you to a place of harmony and happiness. As you smile, others will smile back at you. Smiling is viral and is the best medicine for all your ailments. When we smile, and receive a smile in return, barriers of judgment and condemnation are broken down. The returned smile says, "You are okay." Of course there are many moments you do not feel like smiling, but just try to smile through the shame. The old cliché, "Smile and the world smiles back," is true, and I hope you are encouraged by some of these wise words.

- Peace begins with a smile – *Mother Theresa*
- If the world is a veil of tears, smile 'til rainbows span it – *Lucy Larcom*
- A warm smile is the universal language of kindness – *William Arthur Ward*
- I have witnessed the softening of the hardest hearts by a simple smile – *Goldie Hawn*
- If you smile when no one else is around, you really mean it – *Andy Rooney*

We have learned that acronyms are a great way to remember tools and tips. So here is a nugget around the acronym SMILE:

S   Smile even if you do not feel like it

M   Make a commitment to release the shame

I   Ignite the spark of confidence and joy in your life

L   Live in the light of hope and healing and step out of the darkness of shame

E   Expect the best

EXERCISE:

Practice smiling at yourself every time you pass a mirror.

HEALING IN COMMUNITY

SHATTERING THE SHAME: POLLY'S STORY

I began searching for help approximately five years ago. After three years of not finding help, I was blessed to find Angela's Voice and its support group which was vital in my first steps of healing. It was Angela Williams who took the time to walk over to me and gently tap on that wall and tell me that I had the power and strength to shatter my wall of shame. Volunteering with Angela's Voice is how I received my support and gained the courage to not only work toward my healing, but to dedicate my life to help all survivors find their voice and shatter their wall of shame.

Polly found hope and healing in community. Polly has found reward and continued healing in reaching out to help others. Life has so many challenges, and healing from the shame of child sexual abuse is one we can overcome with some faith, hope, awareness, forgiveness, understanding and new perspective.

Please do not travel this path alone. We encourage you to seek professional help, find a support group or trusted accountability partner to help combat the temptation to stay stuck in the victim role. You can heal, you can thrive and you can be all that you were created to be! Finally – do not give up! Growth and healing does take huge amounts of time and effort, but helpful relationships and good friends are out there – do not give up until you get the support you deserve.

VOICE OF ACTION

SHATTERING THE SHAME: ANGELA'S STORY

I pray that as we expose the millions of toxic emotions due to the shame of sexual assault, together we can find solutions to rid victims of shame. A child can never consent to sexual abuse and the world needs to remove the blame, the shame and the responsibility of sexual abuse from the victim.

As much as we have been silenced, it is time we speak. It is time we amplify our voices to bring about profound change to protect the next generation of children. We have a specific responsibility, knowing intimately the damage of child sexual abuse, to muster the courage to act. We invite you to join the movement and all the many activities of Angela's Voice to protect the next generation of children and help those so profoundly wounded to heal. Sexual abuse has grieved us and you must become an advocate to be a part of the solution. Education is one solution that provides tools and resources to learn more about the issue.

SHATTERING THE SHAME 53

Our hope at Angela's Voice is that these teachings give children a voice of protection and survivors a voice of courage to protect, predict and prevent child sexual abuse. Never be ashamed of the scar, it is just proof that you are stronger than anything that tried to hurt you. Please feel confident that you will shatter the shame of child sexual abuse.

Check out these Additional Healing Resources produced by Angela's Voice:

ANGELA'S VOICE

Angela's Voice is dedicated to developing, distributing, and endorsing valuable resources in the awareness, prevention, and healing of child sexual abuse. The materials, though specific for survivors of child sexual abuse, also benefit any abuse survivor and help protect children by teaching them how to defend themselves from abusive behavior. Founder Angela Williams, MFP, is a survivor-turned-advocate who shares a powerful message of triumph over tragedy by sharing her vulnerable and candid voice about her abuse trauma, her pain, her struggles, and her journey to healing in hopes that it may help other survivors expedite their healing journey.

Williams has devoted years to providing awareness, prevention, and healing programs through her advocacy work. Williams has captivated audiences with her powerful message of triumph over tragedy as a victim of childhood physical and sexual abuse. At age seventeen, she attempted suicide, and that day was the end of her torment and the beginning of a journey to healing. She is a crusader for change and dedicates her life to eradicate child sexual abuse. She holds a master's in forensic psychology with a concentration in child abuse. Williams is a powerful messenger, appearing in national and international news and documentaries. She has been successful in state legislative reform and national policy work and served on the Policy Committee of the National Coalition to Prevent Child Sexual Abuse and Exploitation. She has received numerous accolades and awards for her work, including her collection of books that have valuable lessons for survivors of all ages.

Please follow Angela Williams on social media and contact angelasvoice.com to book a speaking event or interview.

Books by Angela Williams

Loving Me: After Abuse
From Sorrows to Sapphires, Angela Williams's Memoir

Interactive Workbooks—Adults

Healing
Pathway to Healing, Guide to Healing
True Intimacy
Shattering the Shame
Unveiling Child Sexual Abuse

Prevention
Tough Talk to Tender Hearts
The Grooming Mystery
Single Parenting Solutions
Courage to Speak

Children's Books (Ages 5–10)
Gracie Finds Her Voice
Grant Gets His Shield
Gracie and Grant's Big Win
Gracie and Grant's Big Win Coloring Book
Find Your Voice Curriculum Book

Join the Angela's Voice Movement

Take action to break the silence and cycle of Child Sexual Abuse and Exploitation

HELP US SAVE THE NEXT GENERATION OF CHILDREN!

1. Be a Child Advocate
2. Donate at angelasvoice.com
3. Invite Angela Williams to Speak
4. Purchase another Angela's Voice Prevention or Healing Book

Discover more child sexual abuse prevention and healing resources at **angelasvoice.com** and follow angelasvoice in social media.

Instagram @Angelasvoice

Facebook @Angelasvoice

Twitter @Angelasvoice

Linkedin/angelasvoice

Angelasvoice.blogspot.com

Youtube.com/angelakwilliams

www.ingramcontent.com/pod-product-compliance
Lightning Source LLC
Chambersburg PA
CBHW040010080526
44586CB00028B/2948